God is Light

Andrea Joy Moede

Illustrated By **Kimberly Kau**

God is Light © 2019 Andrea Joy Moede.

All rights reserved. No portion of this book may be reproduced in any form without permission from the publisher, except as permitted by U.S. copyright law.

Scriptures taken from the Holy Bible, New International Reader's Version®, NIrV® copyright © 1995, 1996, 1998, 2014 by Biblica, Inc.™ Used by permission of Zondervan. www.zondervan.com The "NIrV" and "New International Reader's Version" are trademarks registered in the United States Patent and Trademark Office by Biblica, Inc.™

ISBN-13: 97-81091291881

First Edition.

Published by The Fullness Thereof

www.AndreaJoy.org

P.O. Box 334

Bulverde, Texas 78163

Illustrations by Kimberly Kau – KimberlyKauStudio@gmail.com

Project Direction & Design by John W. Nichols – www.GodAndYouAndMe.com/BookHelp

Welcome Parents!

I am so honored that you picked up this book for your child! I wrote this little rhyme when our two oldest children (the bash brothers) were quite small. This quest for light (versus dark) seemed to be a good teaching tool, as we were trying to explain to them the basics of discernment and how to guard their hearts. I pray that *God Is Light* will benefit your family in a similar way.

I would also like to invite you to download some beautiful line drawings, which were created as an inspiration from the book's illustrations. I hope that these coloring pages will be yet another tool for you to continue teaching your children about God's Light. Please visit:

www.AndreaJoy.org/God-Is-Light-Coloring-Pages

Offered in love,

Andrea

Special Thanks

To **Kimberly Kau** - Thank you for catching the spiritual vision of this book and giving it a beautiful personality in your uniquely creative way. From our hesitant first conversations, to our brainstorming sessions, to our late-night illustration reviews on facetime - it was such a pleasure getting to know you as we developed this project together! I'm ever so grateful to Holy Spirit for connecting us through Patricia King's mentorship program.

To **John W. Nichols** - I'm extremely appreciative for your help in so many areas - from the fantastic cover design, to the book marketing strategies, to the idea for using line drawings as coloring pages, and everything in between - you have been a tremendous project designer and director. The Kingdom momentum this book generates will be largely due to your incredible efforts!

Dedication

For Owen, Colsten, and Adelyn
our precious children of the day
may you be filled with God's light that leads to life
seeing ever more clearly, always discerning light from dark
that nations will come to your light
and kings to the brightness of your new day

Light is bright

Light is pure

Light makes us

feel secure

God is Light!

You have the fountain of life. We are filled with light because you give us light.

Psalm 36:9

Then He will be like the light of morning at sunrise when there aren't any clouds. He will be like the bright sun after rain that makes the grass grow on the earth.

2 Samuel 23:4

Light creates life

Light makes things new

Light is beautiful,

powerful, and true

God is Light!

Light brings peace
Light brings joy
Light brings hope
for every girl and boy
God is Light!

Here is the message we have heard from him and announce to you. God is light. There is no darkness in him at all.

1 John 1:5

But the way of those who do what is wrong is like deep darkness. They don't know what makes them trip and fall.

Proverbs 4:19

But our enemy brought sin

And sin let darkness in

Darkness makes us

feel afraid,

Our GOOD GOD

never wanted us

to feel this way!

So God made a way

To bring us back to the light

To never again

Live in darkness or fright

God is Light!

You have saved me from death. You have kept me from tripping and falling. Now I can live with you in the light that leads to life.

Psalm 56:13

Jesus spoke to the people again. He said, "I am the light of the world. Those who follow me will never walk in darkness. They will have the light that leads to life."

John 8:12

God sent His Son, Jesus,

To carry all sin

So that we could live

In the light once again

God is Light!

Now clean and forgiven

Washed whiter than snow

Selfless, He saved us

We must let others know

God is Light!

Lord, you are my lamp.
You bring light into my darkness.

2 Samuel 22:29

All of you are children of the light.
You are children of the day.
We don't belong to the night.
We don't belong to the darkness.

1 Thessalonians 5:5

So let's walk in the light

Better yet,

let's run to the light

And become brilliant tools

Of His power and might

God is Light!

And tell all our friends

There is no more night

Jesus is here

Come to His light

God is Light!

There will be no more night. They will not need the light of a lamp or the light of the sun. The Lord God will give them light. They will rule forever and ever.

Revelation 22:5

Questions for Kids!

1. Do you feel happier and safer when it's light or when it's dark? Why do you think that is?

2. Can you tell when something is light or dark? Think of a movie, book, song, story, or place and decide which one it is.

3. Why do you think God wants us to always walk in the light with Him?

4. Have you ever sinned and felt trapped in the dark? What can you do to get back into the light?

5. How can you practice walking in God's light every day?

6. Is there someone you know who needs to hear about Jesus – the light of the world?

7. Do you really believe that you can change the world by shining God's light? Why or why not?

Nations will come to your light.
Kings will come to the brightness of your new day.
Isaiah 60:3

Reviews help us know if we should check out a book. Would you take a few minutes to review this book wherever you purchased it? Thank you for helping *God is Light* bless more people!

Get free Coloring Pages from *God Is Light* at:

www.AndreaJoy.org/God-is-Light-Coloring-Pages

About the Author

Andrea Joy Moede is a busy mom of three who left the accounting and finance world to stay home with the 'triple threat' and found a love of writing in the process. She released her first book, Misunderstood, in 2017. This work, God is Light, is her first children's book.

Andrea is passionate about helping people come into the fullness of both their identity and calling and believes that this is best accomplished by beholding God in all of His fullness first. When not writing, you can catch Andrea busy with some of her favorite things - highly doctored coffee, endorphin inducing workouts, schmaltzy movies, long naps on rainy days, really good Italian food, coaching her kids sports teams, and sitting down with just about any book.

She lives in the San Antonio area with her husband - Austen, their two busy boys, and their equally busy baby girl. They enjoy being a part of what God is doing at Bethel Austin and throughout the hill country. When not enduring the climate of South Texas, they all prefer to escape to the mountains.

Connect with the author at AndreaJoy.org.

About the Illustrator

Kimberly Kau is a passionate lover of Jesus Christ, a wife, and a busy stay at home mother of three extremely cute children. Despite her active schedule, she loves to find time to get in the secret place with the Lord, read the scriptures, discover what is on the Father's heart, and point people towards the freedom and rest that is found in a genuine relationship with Jesus; the Messiah to Israel, to all the Nations, and to all who would call upon His name!

Kimberly is passionate about encouraging others to shake off empty religion, truly seek understanding of the finished work of the cross, and to continually experience the immeasurable greatness of God's power made available through faith.

She also loves to encourage others interested in the creative arts to have confidence in who they were created to be, find their own artistic style, push past all the fear, and simply enjoy the process. She personally enjoys painting, pottery, pen and ink, colored pencil, and teaching art classes.

Connect with the illustrator at KimberlyKauStudio@gmail.com.

About the Book Designer

At the mention of books John W. Nichols ears perk up, he gets a spine-tingling sensation (no pun intended), and he can't help but find out what read is on discussion. With his first computer at twelve years of age, John began writing, and he is an avid reader, always with a stack of books by his bedside and listening to as many audiobooks as possible when working on mindless tasks. When Jesus saved him at the age of twenty, John started reading the best book you could ever read, over and over, recognizing the Holy Bible as a letter from the creator of all things.

He thought one day (when he was old) he might write a book for God. But God thought he should write something sooner, and told John in a prayer session on January 1st, 2016 to write his book. Since then John has not only written and published his own book. He has helped several authors publish theirs as well.

Get help with your book at GodAndYouAndMe.com/BookHelp.